A Musicians
Christmas Recipes

Sung Once

Written by
Lucy Victoria Treloar

Print information available on the last page.

Rev. date: 10/16/2017

To order additional copies of this book, contact:
Xlibris
1-800-455-039
www.xlibris.com.au
Orders@Xlibris.com.au

A Musicians
Christmas Recipes

Sung Once

Written by
Lucy Victoria Treloar

Table of Contents

Elves' Helpers Loosen Socks

1 fireplace
3 kindling logs
16 toy soldiers
110 centimetres of spider silk
4–5 stockings
20 neon lights
mantel

Racing down the chimney flute
Is an investigator's eye,
As together a group attached to spider silk—
What a little spy,
To see if the room can be found
Without a person near.
A glistening little twinkle alerts all those who are intended near.
With some little symbols used like a code transcribed, and clear,

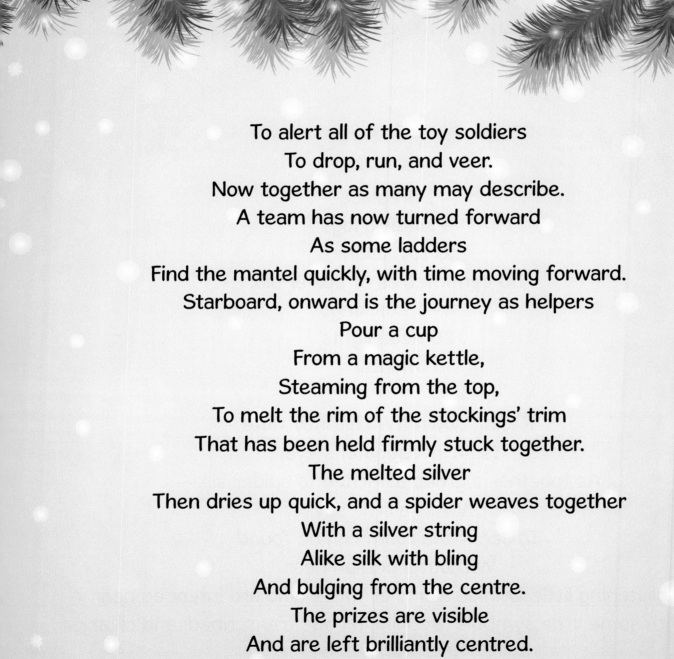

To alert all of the toy soldiers
To drop, run, and veer.
Now together as many may describe.
A team has now turned forward
As some ladders
Find the mantel quickly, with time moving forward.
Starboard, onward is the journey as helpers
Pour a cup
From a magic kettle,
Steaming from the top,
To melt the rim of the stockings' trim
That has been held firmly stuck together.
The melted silver
Then dries up quick, and a spider weaves together
With a silver string
Alike silk with bling
And bulging from the centre.
The prizes are visible
And are left brilliantly centred.

A Dimple and a Waterfall

lagoon
45 logs
7 axes
9 fountain pens
12 babushka dolls
11 presents
3 maracas
4 bunches of green leaves
3 Christmas hampers

A paddle turns a canoe
About
And before your eyes
Is the most majestic sight,
As what is imagined is evidently clear.
A rhythm is heard,

Made by a rumble of dolls,
As they dance about,
Twisting a synchronised beat,
With a drum at their feet.
As they're bursting with energy,
The earth's floor becomes a door,
And a porthole to explore,
And a place to drum a beat aloud,
And a place for everyone to make a shout,
As they know what it's all about.
As this is for them a great world show,
For all the smiles and tears to glow,
As a canoe is then turning to and fro,
With the tempo the ebb and flow.

Fairies Snowboarding in the Sunshine

4 beams of sunshine
71 wakeboards
3 sand castles
4 clouds of vapour
1 rippling blue sky
1 ornamental shield
3 gold bells
16 white candles
a cool breeze

The moonbeams,
Replace the sunshine,
And a cloud is a mist in the twinkling moonlight,
Castles are created by an empire,

And are lost by clouds of vapour white.
Aside of these beams, these rays of sunshine,
Gold bells turn the blue sky bright.
With a gift of balloons, and a breeze of gold,
A golden shield moves to reveal a sight
With music dancing,
And candles entrancing,
And wind to twirl you at your feet,
Moving softly.
The sky is rocking,
As a wakeboard drifts a fairy's feet.

With Stars Shining Around

5 small stars
6 moon beams
4 large crystals
1 horseshoe
1 sphere
1 rocking cradle
11 large stars

A song can be sung,
As a baby is found,
Asleep in a cradle,
With large stars
Above and around.
The cradle is rocking so gently in time,
With large crystals and spheres spinning around and around,
With tunes to be sung to brighten our heart,

As a song is heard and sung from the start,
A lullaby about Christmas to our ears and our hearts.
As is heard,
And then sung,
In this very bright night.

Baubles Patterns Are Stencilled in Crayon

6 crayons
4 tree stencils
3 bell stencils
4 star stencils
3 Santa stencils
4 snowflake stencils
5 rocking horse stencils
4 colour wheels
19 baubles
20 pallets of coloured craft paint

Shadows shading, drawn, stencilled in crayon,
Whilst preparing for the spectacular in store.
As the detail that is imagined

Shapes everything a mind can see.
Stars, bells, and trees
Snowflakes,
Rocking horses,
And great colourful wheels.
Have great potential,
As tracing with the image stamps,
An imagination is found.
As every colourful masterpiece is a glowing
Boundary,
But with a great tall Ferris wheel,
A find.
With Santa's reindeer being helpful helpers,
Slopping with tins of paint,
Using great big radical paint brushes,
That rain all of the paint.
To bring a lot of richness, and vibrant colours,
With no paint to waste.

A rainbow,
A mixer,
Sharpeners and stencils.
And so much time, no haste
As the baubles float and the designs are crafted,
Whilst whistles, bells, and drapes
Fall around, evidently mastered.
With the crayons a lasting trace.

Chimney Sweep Sticks

12 twigs
6 balls of twine
3 dust pans
37 fire poker sets
9 chimney brushes
5 spinning wheels
6 pages of coloured cardboard
gold coins

It was a game of luck,
Not to lose that chance;
Perhaps the reward is as great,
As a spinning wheel that can dance.
Watch as the fire poker is igniting the flame,
To reveal
All of the golden coins that will remain,

Seen through dreamingly, with glitter within the eyes,
A chimney sweeper.
Espy
Some single spindles of coloured thread
Are held brought together in a bind,
Creatively as a masked piece.
And a concealment to be found,
As, hidden within a prize,
Is something that would bring just a smile,
As many creations are around,
Spun into a twine.

Santa Dashes East

1 sleigh
2 reins
43 bells
63 shiny silver balls
16 whistles
7 large Christmas sacks
520 metallic threads
6 arrows
1 pair of binoculars
2 zigzag lines

Drawn on an explorer's map,
Is a known destination,
With a secret stash.
Threadbare,
As whistles confuse the point,
Zigzagging a distraction;

With bells, balls, and stumps.
As the world is seen through the night so well,
With a great pair of binoculars,
And the lens clear as well.
The moon shines a light,
Now caught under a spell.
Where noticeable are the arrows in this night
That then spin the world around,
And are caught in a whirlpool of an imaginable speed,
Spinning around and around and around,
With the reins steering the sleigh as Santa
Abounds
Scattering many hundreds of gifts,
Sprinkling them like confetti rain.
And travelling faster than a shooting star,
This mystery and Santa caught in an orbit,
Of magical white rain,
With the gifts attached with their gift tags,
And somebody's name.

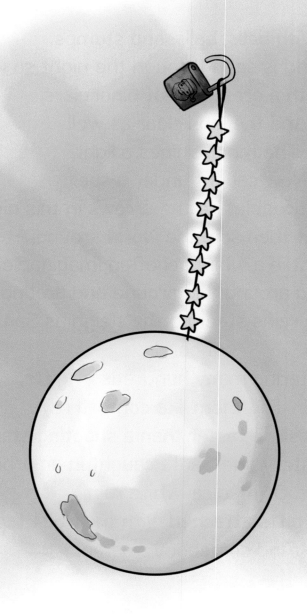

Stars Bright by Night

34 stars
3 moons
5 comets
12 planets
4 millilitres of mercury
air brushes

Our galaxy
Is a wilderness above.
With the diamonds a constellation
And a timeless map.
With planets, comets, and moonshine—
What mystery brightened by the night's sky.
With bright stars a sparkling charm,
As a way, a beginning
Of a fortune-finding tale,

And a story to explore.
Some more,
As explosive is the mention,
Of the history now drawing together,
For all to see.
Well into the distance,
Happiness now dancing in the night's sky.

Golden Chains and Sugar Candy Canes

40 chain links
3 mints
5 humbugs
6 fairy floss
7 strawberries and cream
3 candy apples
32 candy canes
3 gold marbles
4 gold nuggets
4 gold balloons
2 maple syrup twists
1 wooden drizzle

Wrapping a Christmas tree
Around like a cover

To make pretty every last decoration
And smoother
On a green background.
Golden chains,
Placing candy canes,
As this image is just like a maple syrup twist
That spins a marble
To make fairy floss crisp.
With the mints that then link together.
With strawberries and creams,
And a drizzle spinning in the centre;
The spin holds one golden balloon,
That raises the tree to move.
With the eyes weighed down by the movement
As the candy canes
Spring like hooks
And hang on nooks.
Around and about,
The branches of the
Christmas tree.

Metallic Sequins of Rain

4 tins
12 tin cutters
16 metal clips
6 paint pellets
23 glass beads
5 litres of stained-glass paint
2 tracing brushes
jewellery

A shot, a ray of light thrown, electrified into the air.
A spectacular fireworks display.
Lightning too obvious not to stare.
As the tin rumbles and the earth quakes,
And the world shakes,
And paint pallets make
Greater spectrums of colour

Within the darkness of the light.
Are slight hints of another sight,
Of a day can be seen through eyes that glance
At a whirlwind,
Perchance
As turning the world about
Creates the nights spell.
As a magical well
And a wish,
And a way to remember;
With days and sleeps,
Sparkles and treats,
And a new day to us.
Held with amazement and grace,
As this world then becomes a place
To display
Metallic sequins of rain.

Moose's Loose in Strawberry Fields

12 pipes of whipped cream
8 mint leaves
40 coils of barbed wire
62 tulips
600 strawberries
4 kilograms of chocolate
2 raspberry bushes
2 black berry bushes
3 cups of orange syrup
7 apples
24 fences

Trapped inside a fence line
Is a face caught found in despair,
As a quick little look around

Could see all those who stare.
At that, a burst of energy,
A prickle,
Steps then quick.
Was a word there from the memory,
Or just a spring, a nick, and quick zip,
With some upturned tulips,
And comedy,
And some apple syrup and orange twists,
Chocolate cascades like a waterfall.
And a moose whoops his whip.
To put raspberries and some colour,
Along with blackberries to make purple new,
With many mint leaves coiled with barbed wire.
To make a headdress something new,
Like a crown that can be versatile,
And can be worn greatly new,
As anything is possible.
A spirit
Through and through.

With paper aeroplanes aerobatic, and not faltering in this light,
As spinning tops turn with the wind that twirls in the silence.
Not forgotten is this beauty,
A spectacular creation,
And a wish's reliance.
As we see a sparkler waving brightly within this marching band.
And a little songbird is singing, with the cymbals playing each round.
To protect the wrapping paper twirling around,
As to guard is a knight's feat.
Until the night-time finds the day,
Whilst the fireflies help keep the secrets,
Kept from all those far, far away.

Presents under the Tree

40 levers
60 pulleys
11 tightropes
16 train tracks
6 trains
4 ribbons
24 carriages
23 miniature tea sets
62 diamonds
49 jewels

What a character is thought of as a team is created by magic.
With tea sets dancing
And ribbons
Trailing behind a train.
Holding onto jewels that sparkle

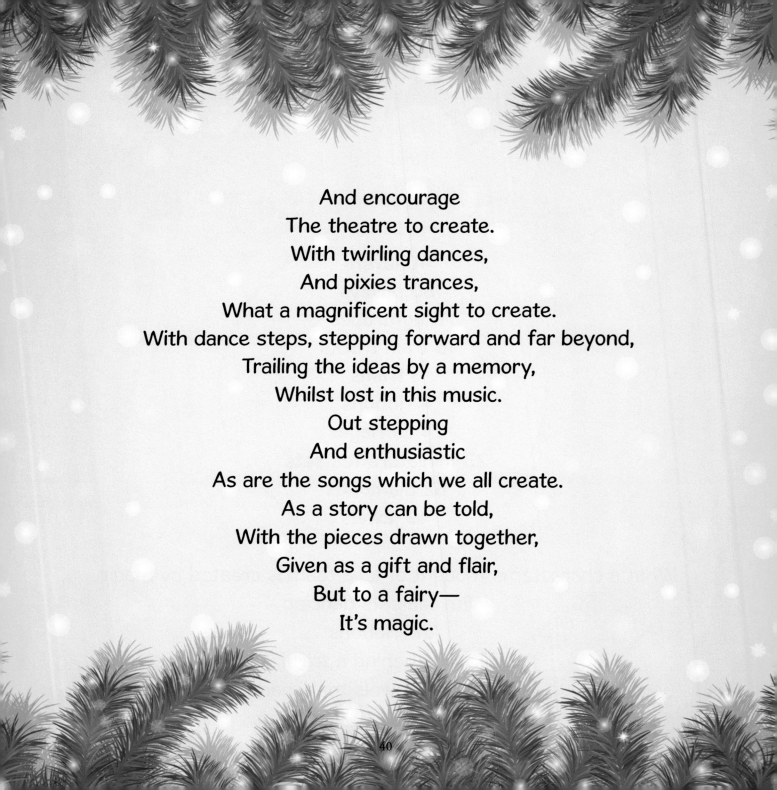

And encourage
The theatre to create.
With twirling dances,
And pixies trances,
What a magnificent sight to create.
With dance steps, stepping forward and far beyond,
Trailing the ideas by a memory,
Whilst lost in this music.
Out stepping
And enthusiastic
As are the songs which we all create.
As a story can be told,
With the pieces drawn together,
Given as a gift and flair,
But to a fairy—
It's magic.

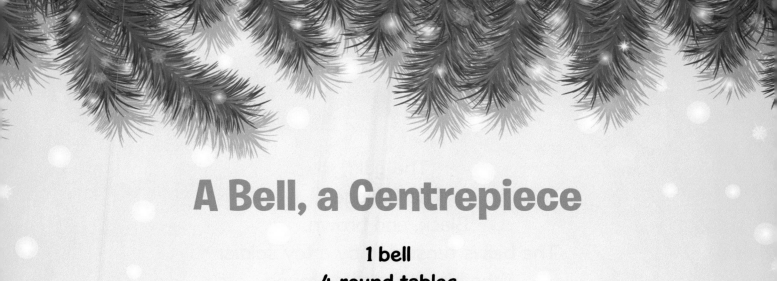

A Bell, a Centrepiece

1 bell
4 round tables
5 table cloths
16 candles
6 springs
3 tuning keys
1 pianola

The ding-dong can be heard, the sound echoing all around;
Has its place in the centre.
Where zigzags and lights are found,
Spectacular where the dashes are bouncing,
Making a strong resounding sound.
With a colourful image made by the silver,

The gold,
The Orange,
Black, and brown.
The bell is tensioned by a toy soldier
Who himself walks around.
Tiny and inside, a beautiful masterpiece easily is a bell to be found.
Within a tiny jewellery box,
And with jewels and valuables,
A piece,
Bound priceless is an eternity.
Wonderfully
At Peace,
Once protected and adorned
By the sound of a whistle blowing
The ding-dong of a bell.
Sounds the cymbals rebounding,
The echo
All around.

Fairies Tied Shoelaces

23 glasses
14 pairs of booties
44 cup cakes
13 pieces of coloured paper
12 mittens
1 gigantic ball of shoelaces
2 silver necklaces
3 diamantes
4 pink buttons
12 baubles

It began with plenty of tinsel,
As well as to expect the feet about a Christmas tree.
And a fairy at rest,
As all is worked out; it is all said and done.
What a memory to accomplish, by finding the heart of a sun.

A silver necklace draws all of the attention,
With the gleam caught in the eyes,
As a glittering, sparkling wrapping spacer—
What such luck to be espied,
Nice things cost plenty.
And precious are the little things:
Like a ball of shoelaces tied together;
With diamantes, pink buttons, baubles, and mittens;
With scrunched pieces of paper,
Pretty and very bright;
And a puzzle that is seen to unravel;
From a great height,
That is hung tall upon a Christmas tree that has been crafted,
By a fairies' writer, known as a light.

Snowmen Float Upstream

12 branches
16 twigs
40 ice bergs
14 oars
32 leaves
5 compasses
6 scarves
24 water tanks
5 rafts
8 hats

A tip of the hat,
A turn to and fro.
Needles and pins,
And twigs and snow.
Marching is now only at tilting speed,

As the wind is a whistle,
As the sound would deplete.
Icebergs
Are thrashed by oars,
Knocked straight out of the way
Whilst water tanks are gathering,
Dragging along the way.
A compass leaves then
The footprints behind,
A never-ending passage.
Wind,
Torques our minds.
As many rafts drift on by,
And the snowmen then retreat
As they then find a greater rhyme to chant by,
And march by feat.

Spinning Tops Zoomed in Shots

2 waterproof cameras
3 fish tanks
4 giant lollipops
7 water pistols
3 red fire engines
12 spinning tops
6 magnifying glasses
5 rulers
6 elves
4 stepladders

Zoom, zoom, zoom, zoom, zoom!
An elf driving a fire engine to the top
Of a peak, a mountain high,
To extend a stepladder and a ruler to the sky.
The fire engine toots,
And a march is found with flutes
As a water tanker becomes a blur.

And unsettled is a puzzled pair,
Dancing about with lollipops
And some skates,
Ice skating
A performance.
But wait—
The sun has melted all of the snow,
And in the distance,
A spinning top is known
To have turned the world upside down
With fish tanks.
A whirlwind,
And mountains reclined.
The gravity zooms the ladders to the side.
And open are the eyes,
As through this crystal ball,
All things are kept secret so well.
But none as mesmerising as what is seen,
Now caught under this spell.

Tinsel Tunes Ruffle Bells and Balls

4 golden wreaths of tinsel
6 blue bells
7 crimson balls
3 violins
3 green wreaths of tinsel
60 bows
5 silver coins
curtains

Bling is the shine.
And ting is the sound.
As we sing, our voices find
The wings to begin a Christmas sight.
As lovingly a tree in the darkness
Glistens in the strongest light,
Whilst a room has begun to create

A carol to be sung so well.
As with the drawing of these pictures forming we find,
Contained,
The music with the sounds of laughter
Remained.
As a large bow as pretty as a harp
Has begun a lilting rhythm
And encapsulated a hidden beauty.
With sonnets, poetry, and a minim,
Drawing upon a staff.
With notes
A musical sign,
As known by the true wonders of a heart,
Is a sound made fonder ruffled by a memory.

Tocks, Clocks, and Stockings

4 grandfather clocks
12 woollen socks
3 hour hands
3 minute hands
4 second hands
3 balls of yarn
4 faces
9 spindles
7 cogs
3 coils of wire
pendulum

Tick-tock, the grandfather clock chimes.
With cogs in a spindle
And with coils of wire.
Just a second, calls a face in the crowd.

The pendulum is rocking,
And the thread is out of time.
As a minute is all the time we need,
As a string can be sewn into a weave,
Turning about within a circle
A mother looking,
Toward her mother:
With a timepiece,
And a smile,
One to not erase.
A big woollen sock is known to have been
Mentioned kindly to fill to the brim
By a fireplace, one magical and rare,
As stuffing a stocking
Is something to share.
Once the hour hand ticks on by,
Fables are with stitches
And the threads are bare,

Use a bookmark to mark
A fictional tale,
One like an idea
That reminded a tale.
Tick-tock—a pendulum swings,
And gravity draws it into the centre.

Wooden Pedals Trail the Train

3 hot air balloons
40 yellow clogs
16 train tracks
6 peddlers' tracks
2 seesaws
3 primary colours
10 litres of paint
6 rocking horses
16 butterflies
10 carnivals
zzzz

Tiptoe, a train whistle blows.
At speed the turn moves faster,
A trip to keep.
Whilst seesaws and heat

Raise the hot air balloons.
Let's pedal faster.
A carnival's master is a rocking horse's tasker.
Let's splash the world with paint,
Pedalling faster.
The butterflies flutter the eyes, and a carnival's sounds engage.
With bright red lights, and green ones too,
With three other colours painting the whistles to,
What can be heard can be seen,
With the rocking horses steer,
And with the music in the ears,
The eyes can brighten bright,
As now far and wide into the distance,
A faint whistle can be heard,
And the train tracks can become blurred.
With the train line track and the curb,
Left behind,
Out of sight,
And now unheard.

Silver Sequins of Rain

40 silver pieces
6 paper clips
11 halos
43 rose petals
23 silver bells
4 coloured rainbows
4 rain clouds
3 map pins
trailing wind

Whoosh—and the wind in a spin
Catches the symmetry, and the pieces collide.
With rain clouds by your side,

A map pin would tip
And hold by the lip
A rose petal among silver bells and chains.
With the illumination sparkling, and shining remarkably
Down as the rain came.
A rainbow is a smile
Drawn to heaven with an open mind,
As a beauty is found within,
And the silver sheets
Remain
As sequins is what became
Of the storm,
To become
Silver sequins of rain.

Printed in the United States
By Bookmasters